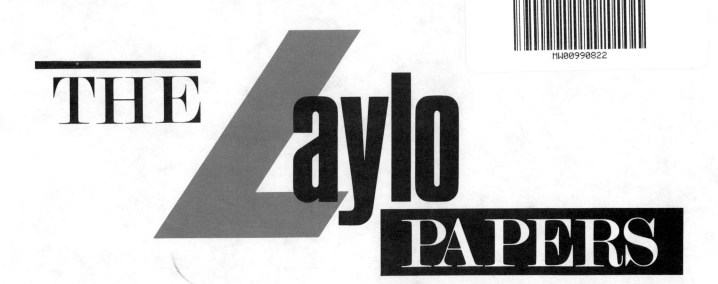

THE Zaylo PAPERS

The Complete Guide to Relationships

By Tim Downs

Foreword by a Really Famous Celebrity

COMMUNICATIONCENTER

Book design: Marketing Communications Group

ISBN: 0-9623125-0-9

Library of Congress Catalog Card Number: 89-090224

This book and the comic strip **Downstown**
would not have been possible without the
devoted efforts of my editor, my copywriter,
my design consultant, my creative consultant,
and my office manager. I married them all.

For Joy.

Table of Contents

Foreword by a Really Famous Celebrity

I don't usually take time away from my duties with Congress to write Forewords to books. But when Tim Downs asked me to contribute this introductory note to his opus, I considered it the greatest honor bestowed upon me since the Nobel Peace Prize.

During my many years in Hollywood, I witnessed first-hand the tremendous need for sensible, practical advice on building good relationships. As a professional football player, I learned what the stress and pace of modern life can do to drive two people apart. In none of the universities where I have taught have I found insights as keen or advice as balanced and workable as that contained in this book.

Nowhere else have I found this kind of wisdom: not in my post-doctoral studies, nor in my many conversations with other literary giants, nor in my consultations with World Leaders whose names you would all recognize.

I'll tell you, boy, this is really a good book. You have my word on it as a philosopher, a scientist, and a great moral leader. Take it from me, the man **Time** magazine once called "about the smartest guy we've ever heard of" in a past issue whose date I cannot now recall.

Yes, I liked this book a lot and I guess I know what I'm talking about.

Sincerely,

A *Really* Successful, Smart, and Famous Celebrity

Introduction

I began writing **Downstown** at the age of 21. My chief concern in life at that age was how to get a date for Friday night. I had other concerns, of course, like how to get a date for *Saturday* night.

I have always been fascinated by relationships. When I began writing my comic strip, it seemed natural to write about the world I lived in. That's why the major characters of **Downstown** are all single men. Let me introduce you to a few of them.

Chuck Laylo

Chuck Laylo, exceptionally smooth and cool man-about-town, is the author of the best-selling book **"The Laylo Papers: The Complete Treatise on Women,"** from which this book takes its name. Chuck knows everything there is to know about women. Just ask him. He always has an angle. He's always on the make. He's never without an excuse.

Eric Johnson

Like many men, Eric Johnson has a great desire to be successful with women. Unfortunately, he has all the suavity of Pee Wee Herman. Johnson's desire to succeed brought him to the master himself, Chuck Laylo. In exchange for lessons about women and relationships, Johnson agreed to act as Laylo's personal administrative assistant.

John

John is not particularly smart, rich, good-looking or ambitious, and he has a heckuva time getting a date. John tries everything, but nothing seems to work. The harder he tries, the worse it seems to get, a reality that is made even more frustrating by the presence of his roommate, Josh.

Josh

Josh is a Renaissance man. He is an artist, writer, philosopher and inventor, convinced that he was born in the wrong century. He could care less about women, and so manages to attract a good number of them, much to the agony of his roommate, John.

Fred

Fred takes a realistic—some would call it cynical—view of life and relationships. His tongue is a laser beam, and he rips through pomposity and vanity without mercy. You can count on Fred to say what no one else would dare to say, which makes him a dangerous but valuable fellow to have around.

A comic strip artist is like a sniper. He hides in the rocks, taking well-aimed shots at the vulnerable areas of the human condition. As Steve Martin said, "Comedy is not pretty." A good comic strip can do a lot more than make people laugh. It can make people *think*.

During the eleven years that I wrote **Downstown** I produced more than 3,000 comic strips, most of which focused on the bizarre world of dating and relationships. Everything I wrote was drawn from a handful of basic convictions about life, human nature, and relationships.

This book is a collection of some of my writing on relationships. At the end of the book, in a section entitled "Thought Bombs," I've included some of the underlying thoughts and convictions that influenced my writing in **Downstown**. I hope they make you think too.

If you have half as much fun reading these strips as I did writing them, then you will have had 50% less fun than I did. Too bad.

1 Self-Image

believe that everyone can have a strong, positive self-image. Even a worthless, insignificant speck of cosmic dust like me.

A poor self-image is often the cause of many relationship problems. Some people have an inflated self-image and appear arrogant and rude. Some people have a negative self-image and find it hard to believe that anyone could love them. Some people have no self-image, like vampires.

Your self-image is not derived from looking at yourself in the mirror. It's derived from looking at yourself in the mirror of other people's eyes. It's the way we think *others* see us.

Unfortunately, "desirability" is usually determined by some very subjective and superficial standards, like the sexiness of your nostrils and whether or not you have a cellular phone.

Certainly the most desirable attribute anyone can have is Beauty. Our evaluation of most people begins and ends right there.

by Tim Downs

HI! I'M LINDA EVANS! I'M 42 AND I NEVER FELT BETTER ABOUT MYSELF.

THAT'S BECAUSE WHEN MOST PEOPLE HIT 40, THEIR LOOKS START TO GO LIKE A CALIFORNIA MUDSLIDE. BUT NOT ME!

I'M MAKING MEGABUCKS BY TELLING YOU THAT EVERY YEAR YOU, TOO, CAN LOOK BETTER AND BETTER!

I'M THE PERFECT SYMBOL FOR A BEAUTY-WORSHIPPING CULTURE THAT'S GROWING STEADILY OLDER.

SO, KEEP DRINKING MY SOFT DRINK AND USING MY HAIR COLOR, AND I'M SURE THAT WHEN YOU'RE 42 YOU'LL LOOK JUST LIKE ME!!

≥ SNICKER SNICKER ≥

THIS MESSAGE WAS BROUGHT TO YOU BY RALPH NADER AND THE "GIVE ME A BREAK" FOUNDATION.

TIM DOWNS

Yes, we can all relate to the agony of being loved only because of our rare and exquisite beauty.

If Beauty is the most desirable attribute anyone can have, the second most desirable must be Talent. Talent includes intelligence, athletic and musical aptitude, and the ability to catch a frisbee behind your back.

The third most desirable attribute for anyone to have is Status. Status is the impression of being Somebody Important and is one of the chief pursuits of our culture.

Of course, there are very few genuinely important people in our society. Not everyone can be a Dr. Joyce Brothers. The rest of us are left building our own significance, sometimes wishing that we were someone else.

In my humble and accurate opinion, our superficial standard of Desirability is epitomized by the Miss America Pageant. Your opinion of the Miss America Pageant is determined by which side of the runway you're on. The contestants see themselves as talented performers, fielding questions on current world problems. The audience sees them as hot-looking ladies in great suits, mumbling something about caring for beached whales.

My critics have pointed out to me that the Miss America Pageant is a legitimate contest of talent and achievement.

All I can say is, Beethoven never performed in a swimsuit.

Since the standard of Desirability is constantly before us, each of us is keenly aware of his deficiencies. Very few people look like Tom Cruise or Kim Basinger. The rest of us are left wishing we did. Frankly, I would be happy if I looked like Kim Basinger, though my wife would find the adjustment difficult.

We pretend to be what we think others are looking for. We begin to wear masks. We wear beauty masks, masks of knowledge and intelligence, and masks of importance. The problem is this: when you enter a relationship, how do you know what you're really getting?

THE RISING SUN FINDS THE DAWN PATROL AWAITING ANOTHER WOMAN TO FETCH HER MORNING PAPER.

IN THE CLEAR LIGHT OF DAWN, YOU FIND OUT WHICH ONES POSSESS *TRUE* BEAUTY!

AHA!!

YOU ALSO FIND OUT WHICH ONES POSSESS DOBERMANS.

KAREN GOODALL IS ABOUT TO FETCH HER MORNING PAPER. SHE WILL HAVE NO MAKEUP, NO BLOW-DRIED HAIR, NO STYLISH CLOTHES...

AND THE *DAWN PATROL* WILL BE WAITING TO CATCH A GLIMPSE OF HER *TRUE APPEARANCE!*

SO THIS IS HOW YOU LOOK!!

YAA!! WHO *IS* THAT?!

ALWAYS STRIKE FROM OUT OF THE SUN.

ANOTHER SILENT DAWN, ANOTHER _____ FOR THE DAWN PATROL.

ANY MINUTE NOW AN UNSUSPECTING WOMAN _____ MORNING PAPER, AND...

AHA!! GREASY HAIR, BAGGY EYES AND TOAD BREATH!!

SCRATCH ONE _____

LUCKY SHOT!!

13

Downstown

by Tim Downs

ALL RIGHT, LET'S BEGIN.

TONIGHT'S SEMINAR IS FROM CHAPTER SEVENTEEN OF THE LAYLO PAPERS: "CAVEAT EMPTOR — LET THE BUYER BEWARE!"

BEFORE MAKING COMMITMENTS, GENTLEMEN, BE CERTAIN OF WHAT YOU ARE GETTING.

THIS IS LISA, OUR "BEAUTY UNMAKE OF THE MONTH." AS YOU CAN SEE, SHE IS A FLAWLESS BEAUTY.

LET'S BEGIN BY REMOVING THE EYEBROW PENCIL, LIP GLOSS, AND BLUSHER.

NOW WE'LL REMOVE EYE-SHADOW, MASCARA, EYE-LASHES, POWDER, LIP LINER...

NEXT THE SHADOWS AND HIGHLIGHTS: THE CHEEK HOLLOWS, THE JAWBONE, THE SIDES OF THE NOSE...

GASP!!

HOLD ON, WE'VE STILL GOT THREE LAYERS OF FOUNDATION.

At some time in life, we've all been evaluated by our beauty, talent and status. Most of us know what it feels like to come up short. It hurts. And it affects the way we respond to each other in relationships.

Everyone knows the standard of Desirability is superficial, unfair and often downright cruel. The odd thing is that we pass it on. We use the same standard to evaluate our children.

Wouldn't it be great if we could give them a break?

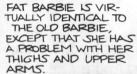

It seems to me that there are two ways I can build a strong, positive self-image.

The first way is to replace the old standard of Desirability with a new one that would let me win. I could learn to see myself in a different way. I could adopt a standard that is honest, fair and unchanging. I could recommend that standard to others.

The second option is to simply meet the existing standard. You can look like Mel Gibson, be built like Arnold Schwarzenegger, and think like Stephen Hawking.

This can be difficult. I mean, it could take *weeks*. And most of the time, it requires a great deal of foresight and planning to accomplish it.

You have to choose your parents carefully.

2 The Search

Adisillusioned young woman once wrote to Dear Abby complaining about the quality of the men she was meeting in singles' bars. Abby wrote back, "You don't catch trout in a herring barrel."

It was one of those profound, life-changing quotations that I rank right up there with the words of Anthelme Brillat-Savarin: "A dessert without cheese is like a beautiful woman with only one eye." Pithy, but it doesn't help a lot. Where *do* you catch trout?

The problem is that trout don't come in barrels. Fishing takes a lot of time and patience, and you have to wear a funny hat. That's why a lot of folks decide to save time and just bob for herring. At least it's *fish*, right?

No one minds catching a fish that's too small or the wrong kind; at least there's encouragement to keep trying. They just don't want to pull up a beer can, an old tire or a '57 Chevy.

by Tim Downs

GANGWAY!!

HA! YOU MISSED ME!

OH YEAH?! WELL I'D RATHER GO OUT WITH AN EAST GERMAN BORDER GUARD, TOO!!

GO AHEAD, SEND ME THE BILL FOR YOUR DRESS! I'LL SEND IT BACK!!

WHAT ARE YOU DOING TO MY TIRES?! YOU'LL HEAR FROM MY LAWYER ABOUT THIS!!

SLAM!

HEY JOSH, HOW COME YOU NEVER GO OUT ON DATES?

The hardest thing about a relationship is just getting started. It's The Search. Not necessarily The Search for Mr./Ms. Right, just for Mr./Ms. Acceptable, a bipedal hominid who doesn't read Shirley MacLaine.

They're not easy to find.

There seem to be some things that work against us in The Search for Mr./Ms. Acceptable. Some of them are cultural; Some of them are environmental; the fact that you mousse your hair with Pennzoil doesn't help either.

Certainly, part of the problem comes from the pace of modern life. A moving target is harder to hit on.

Can we talk? Part of the problem might be you. Remember the Christmas Party, when you ate three pounds of garlic dip? You yawned and your date's eyelashes fell out.

Yes, Virginia, there is a Grapevine, and your reputation preceeds you.

24

One of the things that proves helpful in The Search is a thorough knowledge of the nature and customs of the opposite sex. Believe it or not, this is possible. It should be noted that men and women *are* members of the same species, though certain women I have met believe that men evolved from a type of bathtub fungus.

A knowledge of the opposite sex allows one to search more quickly, sensitively and accurately.

Downstown by Tim Downs

THAT WAS A GOOD RUN, JOHNSON.

LET'S STOP OFF HERE. I WANT TO SAY HI TO JULIA.

SHOULDN'T WE GO HOME AND SHOWER FIRST, SIR?

NAAH! WOMEN THINK MEN ARE VERY SEXY WHEN THEY SWEAT.

ARE YOU SURE ABOUT THAT, SIR?

JOHNSON. DO I KNOW WOMEN OR DO I KNOW WOMEN?

HI, CHUCK! OH, GROSS ME OUT!

HI BABE. HOW 'BOUT A LITTLE HUG?

GET AWAY FROM ME! OH, GAG! LET GO, I THINK I'M GOING TO BE SICK!

CLEAR THE BATHROOM! JOAN, START THE SHOWER! DEBBIE, BURN THESE CLOTHES FOR ME!

SHE LOVED IT.

Downstown

by Tim Downs

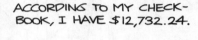

There is a wise old saying: "In relationships, the key is not in *finding* the right person, but in *being* the right person." Dear Abby herself might have said this, on a good day.

If this proverb is true, then our concept of The Search has to be expanded. It means we can't simply *look* for Mr./Ms. Acceptable. We also have to spend some time *becoming* acceptable ourselves.

You will find, like Chuck Laylo, that there is no substitute for an attitude of honesty, sensitivity and genuine unselfishness.

by Tim Downs

DING DONG

MS. NEY BAILEY? I HAVE A RATHER LARGE PACKAGE TO DELIVER TO YOU.

WHO IS IT FROM?

THE SENDER IS LISTED AS A MR. CHUCK LAYLO.

IS IT ABOUT THIS BIG? UNUSUALLY HEAVY? WITH SMALL AIRHOLES IN IT?

HOW DID YOU KNOW?

THAT TURKEY TRIED THE SAME THING LAST YEAR.

I BEG YOUR PARDON?

LISTEN, THERE'S BEEN A MISTAKE. I'M AFRAID THE PACKAGE HAS BEEN DELIVERED TO THE WRONG ADDRESS.

HERE, LET ME GIVE YOU THE CORRECT ADDRESS.

WHO THE HECK ARE YOU?!

31

To paraphrase Dear Abby: "You don't catch trout in a herring barrel. But if *you're* a herring, what would you want with a trout?"

Or how about this: "You don't find trout in a herring barrel, you find them in the super-market next to the halibut." I'm not sure what that means, but I believe it contains a Great Truth of Life.

Having milked the fishing analogy as much as is humanly possible, it's time to go on to the next chapter.

3 The Approach

It's a boring party. No one looks interesting. In the corner is a rather large woman in black stretch pants. She looks like a water balloon with legs. Standing by the buffet table is a woman who is a health food evangelist, warning people about additives. A woman about your mother's age smiles from across the room.

Suddenly, you see her. A *goddess*! She is a *vision*! Everything you ever *wanted* in a woman, and—can it be?—she's *alone*! Without even thinking you stride up to her, pimento spread dribbling down your chin. She turns and looks full in your eyes. Instantly, your brain becomes a black hole. You begin to stutter.

"Uh . . . haven't I . . . seen you alone here . . . often?"

Your neck turns crimson red. You begin to laugh like a donkey. She rolls her eyes, and gives you a look that reaches down your throat and tears out your ego.

Nice going.

Nothing in life is quite as hard as thinking of those first few words, with the possible exception of leaving a message on a telephone answering machine. One of my characters, Chuck Laylo, seemed to have a creative flair for approaching the opposite sex. Maybe you can pick up some ideas from him.

Downtown by Tim Downs

GOOD MORNING, MADAM.

I'M HERE TODAY TO INTRODUCE THE MOST REMARKABLE COUPON BOOK OF ITS KIND.

INTRODUCING THE "CHUCK LAYLO GOLDEN CHECK BOOK."

SUPPOSE THERE'S A BIG PARTY COMING, AND YOU DON'T HAVE A DATE. NO PROBLEM!

JUST TAKE OUT THE "FREE DATE" COUPON! GOOD ANY DAY EXCEPT WEEKENDS AND HOLIDAYS.

OR, SUPPOSE IT'S A LONELY SUMMER EVENING AND YOU LONG FOR A MAN'S POWERFUL ARMS AROUND YOU...

GET OUT OF HERE!!

WOMEN ARE HIGHLY RESISTANT TO NEW PROMOTIONAL CONCEPTS.

Since I created Chuck Laylo, people naturally assume that I share Chuck's knack for introductions. I do. With several hours of preparation and time for rewrites, there's no *limit* to what I can come up with.

Now, doing it on the *spot*, that's another matter. Unfortunately, life seems to call for quite a bit of spontaneity. That's when it gets hard. And, to be fair, it didn't always work, even for Chuck Laylo.

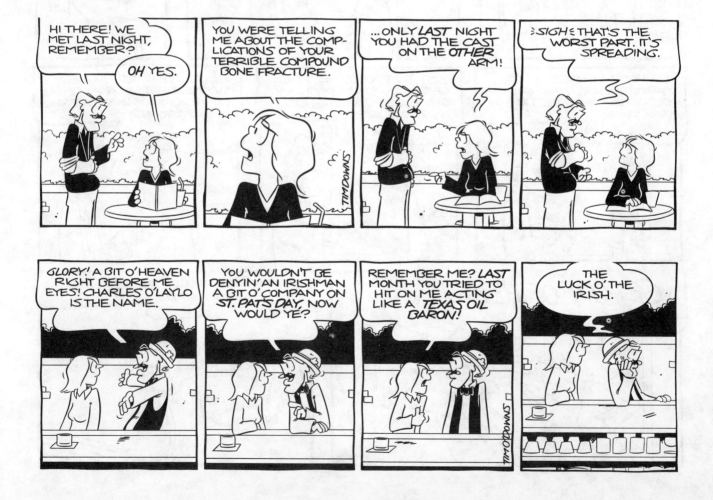

Can the art of The Approach be learned? Chuck Laylo thought so. He had an apprentice named Eric Johnson. Johnson served as Chuck's administrative assistant in exchange for lessons on relating to women. Laylo did his best to teach him to be smooth, cool, confident and irresistible.

Somehow, Johnson always got it wrong. But somehow, in getting it wrong, he ended up getting it right.

by Tim Downs

THERE SHE IS, JOHNSON.

OKAY, NOW, WHAT'S YOUR OPENING LINE?

"HI! I'VE BEEN HOPING ALL EVENING TO GET A CHANCE TO TALK WITH YOU..."

NO, NO, NO!

DON'T GIVE HER THE UPPER HAND! LET HER KNOW *YOU'RE* GIVING *HER* A *BREAK!*

"HI! I COULDN'T HELP NOTICING YOU, YOU SURE STAND OUT FROM THE OTHER WOMEN."

NO, NO, NO!

DON'T TELL HER SHE'S *BEAUTIFUL* OR SHE'LL THINK SHE'S TOO GOOD FOR YOU!

THIS IS YOUR LUCKY NIGHT, BAGFACE.

41

by Tim Downs

OKAY, JOHNSON, THERE'S THE TARGET.

NOW WHEN YOU WALK UP TO HER, JOHNSON, THIS IS WHAT YOU SAY...

EXCUSE ME, SIR. DO YOU THINK MAYBE I COULD TRY IT BY MYSELF THIS TIME?

WELL, IF YOU WANT TO TAKE A CHANCE ON GOOFING IT UP, GO AHEAD!

HI. I'M ERIC. YOU SEEM LIKE A VERY NICE PERSON. WOULD YOU LIKE TO TALK?

THAT IS THE MOST REFRESHING INTRODUCTION I HAVE HEARD IN YEARS. NO LINES, NO PLOYS...

HOW EVER DID YOU LEARN TO BE SO GENUINE?

FOR ONE THING, HE HAD A GREAT TEACHER.

One of my earliest characters was a young man named John. John did not have the best of luck with women, to put it mildly.

However, necessity is the mother of invention, and John's failures only forced him to become more creative and elaborate in his attempts to meet women. Sometimes he simply used the Direct approach.

Sometimes he appealed to the woman's sense of charity.

Then there was the Spiritual approach.

Often, he resorted to different versions of what I would call the K-TEL approach.

GOOD EVENING. I'M WITH JOHN'S ESCORT SERVICE.

I DIDN'T CALL FOR AN ESCORT!

YOU MISUNDERSTAND. YOU HAVE BEEN SELECTED AS THE *WINNER* OF OUR *BIG SPRING GIVEAWAY!*

AMONG THE PRIZES YOU HAVE WON IS AN EVENING WITH *JOHN HIMSELF!*

GET LOST.

I DIDN'T EVEN GET TO TELL HER ABOUT THE FREE SPICE RACK.

LADIES! YOUR ATTENTION OVER HERE, PLEASE!

DON'T MISS THE BARGAIN OF A LIFETIME!

RIGHT HERE! FOR THE NEXT FIVE MINUTES ONLY!

BLUE LIGHT SPECIAL.

NO WAY WILL I GO OUT WITH YOU!

CONGRATULATIONS! YOU ARE THE *1,000TH WOMAN* TO TURN ME DOWN!!

THESE ARE JUST A *PART* OF THE *SHOWER OF PRIZES* YOU HAVE WON, *STARTING* WITH...

DINNER FOR TWO (WITH ME) AT *LA POUBELLE!*

NO WAY!

FOR A MINUTE, I THOUGHT WE HAD HER THERE.

Sometimes he used the Reassuring approach.

And, of course, there was always Desperation.

Use the approach that works best for you. And, if all else fails, I suppose you can always be honest.

The Approach was hard for John. It is for everyone. I suppose there's only one thing harder than meeting someone.

Waiting around to be met.

by Tim Downs

I'VE ASKED *HUNDREDS* OF WOMEN FOR A DATE, AND I'VE *ALWAYS* USED SOME KIND OF *SCHEME* OR *PLOY*...

THIS TIME I'M JUST GOING TO BE *HONEST.*

I'M A LONELY, SINGLE GUY ISOLATED IN A COLD, FAST-MOVING, IMPERSONAL WORLD. I'D LIKE SOME *COMPANY.*

I *KNOW* I DON'T LOOK LIKE DON JOHNSON. BUT I WOULD *LISTEN* TO YOU. I WOULD *CARE* ABOUT YOU. I WOULD *RESPECT* YOU.

OH, JOHN! ¿SNIFF¿ I'VE *NEVER* HAD A MAN BE SO *VULNERABLE* AND *HONEST* WITH ME! IT MAKES ME FEEL THAT *I* CAN BE HONEST AND VULNERABLE, *TOO!*

I'M A SOCIALLY CONSCIOUS WOMAN WHO WOULD RATHER DIE THAN BE *SEEN* WITH YOU.

TIM DOWNS

4 Rejection

There is a story told of Thomas Edison. Edison was working hard to discover a substance that could serve as a filament in his new electric light bulb. In the process, Edison unsuccessfully tested 4,500 substances. (This number varies from 12 to 450,000 in different versions of the story, depending on the enthusiasm of the one telling the story. I use 4,500.)

A friend asked him how it was going. Edison told him that he had so far run 4,500 experiments without success. His friend exclaimed, "Why, then you haven't learned a thing!" Edison replied, "On the contrary. I've learned 4,500 things that don't work." And with that, he invited his friend to sit down and relax on his newest invention, the electric chair.

The moral of the story is: You can make the best of failure, but it still hurts.

Unfortunately, failure is a part of relationships. Anyone who attempts a relationship runs the risk of rejection. Rejection takes many forms, from a simple snub or cold shoulder to being pushed from a moving car.

Sometimes rejection is like being massaged with a shovel.

by Tim Downs

Sometimes rejection is more subtle. It can be polite, even thoughtful.

Rejection can be merciful and occur early in a relationship. It's still frustrating, but in the long run it's less painful.

Downstown

by Tim Downs

WHOA!

"EXCUSE ME. HAVEN'T WE MET BEFORE?"

"NO," SHE REPLIES, "I'M SURE I WOULD HAVE REMEMBERED."

"STRANGE. I FEEL AS THOUGH I *KNOW* YOU." SHE PAUSES. "THAT'S ODD. WHEN I LOOK IN YOUR EYES, I FEEL IT, TOO."

"I'M SORRY," I STAMMER, "YOU MUST THINK I'M AWFULLY FORWARD." "NO, PLEASE!" SHE INTERRUPTS, "WE MUSN'T LET THIS OPPORTUNITY ESCAPE US!"

"I... I SUPPOSE YOU ALREADY HAVE PLANS FOR TONIGHT." HER HAND REACHES FOR MINE. "I DID... BUT NOT ANYMORE."

> AHEM < EXCUSE ME, HAVEN'T WE MET BEFORE?

IF WE DID, I'M SURE IT WAS BRIEF.

THAT'S THE TROUBLE WITH WOMEN, THEY NEVER WORK FROM THE SCRIPT.

Sometimes rejection takes the form of a nagging suspicion that your partner would rather be somewhere else.

Or worse, with *someone* else.

People respond to rejection in different ways. Some respond like Charlie Brown, becoming shy, quiet and introspective. Others respond like Freddy Krueger in "Nightmare on Elm Street," which is extremely messy.

It's strange that rejection can produce such a range of responses, from anger to self-pity to shyness.

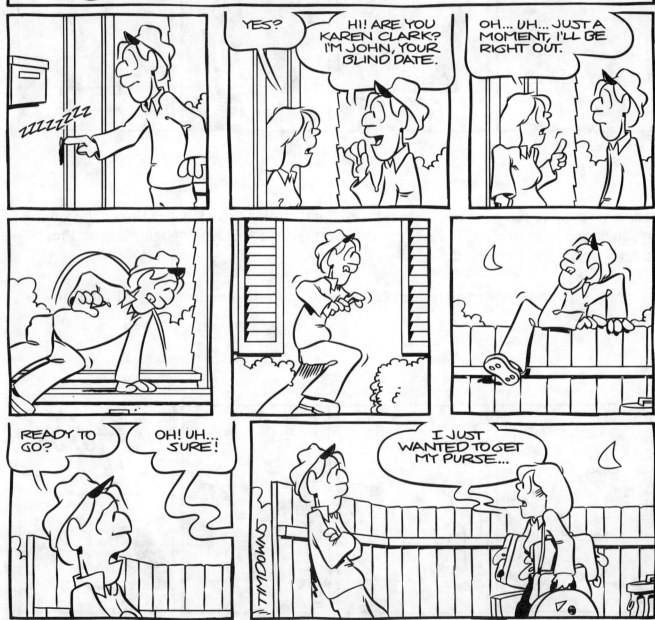

63

Constant rejection can lead to desperation, as it often did for John.

Rejection can even make you a little mean.

Y'knowwutuhmean?

If rejection teaches us anything, it should teach us how to reject someone else without ripping the toupee off his self-esteem. After all, sometime *you're* the one who has to do the breaking up.

Chuck Laylo had a lot of experience with rejection. To him, breaking up was a kind of art form.

Usually Laylo preferred to make it quick and clean.

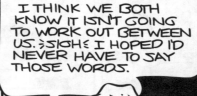

Regardless of the method he used, Chuck always recognized that the best policy is to be open, honest and, above all, sensitive.

It was the immortal Dizzy Dean who said, "What goes around, comes around." Rejection can be like a riccocheting bullet. Be careful how you hand it out. *You* could get hurt in the process.

Even Chuck Laylo learned that.

5 Communication

You're speaking with a friend. As you speak, your friend's eyes begin to dart periodically from your eyes to a point on your face about half an inch to the left of your mouth. His eyes now become hypnotically fixed on that point.

You consider your options. You could simply shift half an inch to the left and bend slightly at the knees. You could make a witty comment, like "I'm saving that for a snack." You could comment on the Stegosaurus that just walked past the window, hoping he would turn for a moment.

Instead you gesture casually as you speak. Your hand inconspicuously brushes your face, as if to scratch a minor itch. Your friend's eyes are now fixed on the tip of your nose.

I *hate* it when that happens.

One thing is for sure. Your friend didn't hear a word you were saying. There was a lot of talk, but no communication.

That situation describes most relationships; a lot of talk, but no communication. If there is a single biggest source of problems in relationships—especially in marriage—it's the way we communicate.

Throughout history, many Great Minds have observed that we have two ears but only one mouth; perhaps we should listen twice as much as we speak. Of course, we also have two legs but only one back. Should we walk twice as much as we lie down?

This kind of question has kept me from the company of the Great Minds.

I have to admit, I think they have a point. The greatest problem in our communication is that we just don't listen.

by Tim Downs

Once you have a listener, the ball is in your court. Now it's your responsibility to articulate clearly what you think and feel. That's harder than it sounds.

In relationships, the problems often don't come from things you say. They come from things things you *don't* say.

Have you ever noticed how deafening silence can be?

by Tim Downs

I grew up in front of a TV set. People watch TV in different ways. Some people are passive viewers. They are able to watch TV, eat, read and remove a gall bladder at the same time.

I am an active viewer. When the TV is on, nothing else in the universe exists. I am oblivious to telephones, conversations, and earthquakes smaller than 4.2 on the Richter scale. I believe television has influenced the way I think. Sometimes my dreams have credits. No kidding.

For me, TV has a way of replacing communication; for some, it has a way of replacing life.

I believe that divorces seldom occur because of major philosophical differences between husband and wife. It's very rare, after 20 years of marriage, for a woman to look at her husband and say, "You're a *Republican*?"

That's too easy. Marriages more often break down because of of toxic waste. It's a residue of bitterness caused by communication filled with cuts, insults, put-downs and sarcasm.

One of my earliest characters was a man named Fred. To put it simply, he was the Master of Sarcasm. Most of the time, he appeared as a waiter.

Downstown by Tim Downs

I WANT TO KNOW ABOUT THE REAL *YOU*, FRED.

TELL ME HOW YOU'RE *FEELING.*

FINE.

IS THAT ALL YOU CAN SAY? FINE? WHY CAN'T *GUYS* EXPRESS *THEMSELVES?* WHY CAN'T...

I FEEL ANXIETY ABOUT AN UNCERTAIN ECONOMY. I FEEL UNEASY ABOUT MY ROLE AS A MAN.

I FEEL WORRIED THAT THE QUESTION OF MARRIAGE WILL COME UP BETWEEN US WHEN I'M NOT READY FOR IT.

I FEEL INSECURE BECAUSE YOU'RE SMARTER THAN I AM. I FEEL AFRAID OF AGING, AND THAT I'LL NEVER AMOUNT TO ANYTHING.

TIMDOWNS

WELL, I'M GLAD YOU'RE FINE.

As you read Fred's remarks in the preceding strips, you probably did not say to yourself, "Yes, that kind of sarcasm is really uncalled for." More likely, you were thinking, "I can *use* that one!" If you do, of course, there is the matter of a royalty.

Sarcasm has become an American art form. I love sarcasm. For eleven years I began each day by sticking my tongue in a pencil sharpener. I made a living out of it. So did Fred.

That last strip is one of my favorites. It always reminded me that there are some places where sarcasm just doesn't belong. A good thing can cause problems in the wrong place, like a screen door on the space shuttle.

I try to leave my sarcasm at the office when I come home at night. I recommend it. So does my wife.

6 The Ego

There is a philosophy known as Solipsism. It's the belief that you are the center of the universe. You are the only being who actually exists. Everyone else is merely the product of your imagination. If you were to cease to exist, the universe would cease to exist also.

I believe this. I find it very bothersome that you believe it, too. To make matters worse, there are five billion other beings on our planet who seem to believe it also. Someone must be wrong.

Maybe all of us are wrong. Inside each of us, there is Something that wants to give us an exaggerated sense of our importance. It wants to be the center of things. It wants to be applauded, honored, raised up. Like the Blob, it exists only to grow. I think Gore Vidal captured the essence of it when he said, "It is not enough to succeed; others must fail."

I simply call it the Ego.

I created the character of Chuck Laylo in 1975. His one distinguishing characteristic was that he had an Ego the size of the starship Enterprise, with better weaponry.

by Tim Downs

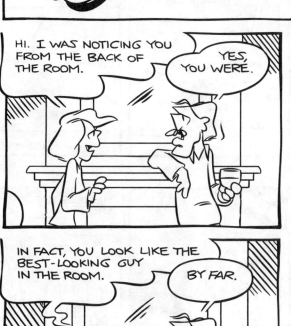

by Tim Downs

YOU LOOK LIKE YOU STAY IN PRETTY GOOD SHAPE, CHUCK.

THAT'S TRUE.

MY BODY IS A TEMPLE.

FEEL FREE TO WORSHIP.

AS THE CROWD LOOKS ON, CHUCK LAYLO TESTS THE DIVING BOARD IN PREPARATION FOR A DIVE.

HE FROWNS IN DISDAIN. THE BOARD IS INFERIOR. THE TENSION IS ALL WRONG.

THE *GREAT* DIVER COMPENSATES FOR THESE VARIABLES WHEN HE DIVES.

THE NOT-SO-GREAT DIVER NEVER INTENDED TO GO OFF THE BOARD ANYWAY.

DO YOU HAVE A *REASON* FOR STANDING ME UP LAST NIGHT, LAYLO?!

DO I HAVE A *REASON*?! DO YOU THINK I'D DO SOMETHING LIKE THAT WITHOUT A *REASON*?! OF *COURSE* I HAVE A REASON!

WHAT IS THE REASON?!

OH, WELL, THAT'S AN ENTIRELY DIFFERENT QUESTION.

by Tim Downs

by Tim Downs

The Ego is something like an inner tube; it can be inflated and deflated. Psychologists believe it may even have a little rubber valve on the side.

An inflated Ego serves several useful purposes. First, it helps you to hold a much higher opinion of yourself than less discerning people do.

Second, it helps to fill the gap between the person you are and the person you wish you could be.

An inflated Ego is capable of taking the most mundane activity and turning it into an accomplishment of almost Herculean proportions.

This accounts for professional football, the Vice-Presidency and Vanna White.

IT WAS A STARK, GREY, SILENT MORNING. WE HAD THE SPOOR OF A SMALL, ISOLATED HERD. THE LAND ROVER LURCHED TO A HALT.

I SWEPT THE BROWN OCEAN OF BUSHVELDT WITH THE SIGHT ON MY BOLT-ACTION MAUSER.

TIM DOWNS

IT'S A YOUNG BULL, JOHNSON. GIVE ME THE .460 WEATHERBY.

YES, BWANA.

I NEEDED STOPPING POWER. I CHOSE THE EVANS .470 NITRO EXPRESS.

THIS LITTLE BABY'S TWIN BARRELS HOLD 10,000 POUNDS PLUS OF MUZZLE-ENERGY PERSUASION.

INTO MY POCKET I DROPPED A FIVE-PACK OF 300 GRAIN, COPPER-JACKETED DEATH.

GOSH I LOVE THAT KIND OF TALK.

TIM DOWNS

SIR, ARE YOU SURE YOU NEED THAT BIG OF A GUN? WE'RE ONLY HUNTING RABBITS!

ONLY RABBITS?!

JOHNSON, ONE OF THE BIGGEST MYTHS OF NATURE IS THAT OF THE "HARMLESS RABBIT"!

HAVE YOU EVER SEEN AN ENRAGED, WOUNDED RABBIT TURN ROGUE?!

NO, SIR.

WELL, LUCKY FOR YOU I NEVER MISS.

TIM DOWNS

THERE IS A LULL IN THE HUNT. THE HUNTERS REST BY A CLEARING IN THE LONG GRASS.

IN TIMES LIKE THESE, HUNTERS SPEAK OF OTHER DAYS, OTHER HUNTS, OTHER KILLS.

TIM DOWNS

I RAN OVER A SKUNK ONCE.

THE FIRST ROUND LAY READY IN THE CHAMBER, DEADLY AS A MAMBA IN ITS HOLE.

THE SKILLED HUNTER'S FINGER TIGHTENED ON THE TRIGGER, AWAITING THE TELLTALE PAUSE BETWEEN HIS HEARTBEATS...

POW!

TIM DOWNS

OH, SHUT UP.

YES, BWANA.

BLAM! BLAM! BLAM!

AH! A GOOD, CLEAN KILL! SEND THE BOY FOR THE TROPHY, JOHNSON.

...THE TROPHY?...

TIM DOWNS

UM... CHUCK, WHY DO YOU HAVE A COTTON BALL STUCK ON THAT PLAQUE?

They say an Optimist is someone who jumps off a building, and as he passes each floor he shouts, "Everything's okay so far!" An inflated ego is like that. It just doesn't hear bad news.

When an inner tube is overinflated, it explodes. When the Ego is overinflated, it becomes virtually puncture-proof.

Downstown

by Tim Downs

CHUCK! CHUCK LAYLO! DO YOU REMEMBER ME? MARY KARPINSKI!!

OF COURSE I REMEMBER YOU!

AS I RECALL, ONCE UPON A TIME YOU WERE CRAZY ABOUT ME.

YEAH, WELL, THAT WAS A LONG TIME AGO.

YOU KNOW WHAT THEY SAY... ONCE YOU'VE GOT THE DISEASE, YOU NEVER GET OVER IT.

NOT IN MY CASE.

SURE, SURE. AND I SUPPOSE THIS WAS JUST A CHANCE MEETING TODAY?

LAYLO, YOU'RE IMPOSSIBLE.!!

DO YOU KNOW WHAT I'VE BEEN DOING SINCE THE LAST TIME I SAW YOU? I MET A GUY, GOT MARRIED, AND HAD TWO KIDS'!

THERE'S NO END TO THE LENGTHS SHE'LL GO TO TO MAKE ME JEALOUS.

If you took an inner tube to the ocean floor, it would compress to a fraction of its normal size. This occurs for reasons that I will not take the time to explain, since it would require me to return to college.

When an inflated Ego is taken out into the real world, it often reduces in size, too. It can be an unpleasant experience.

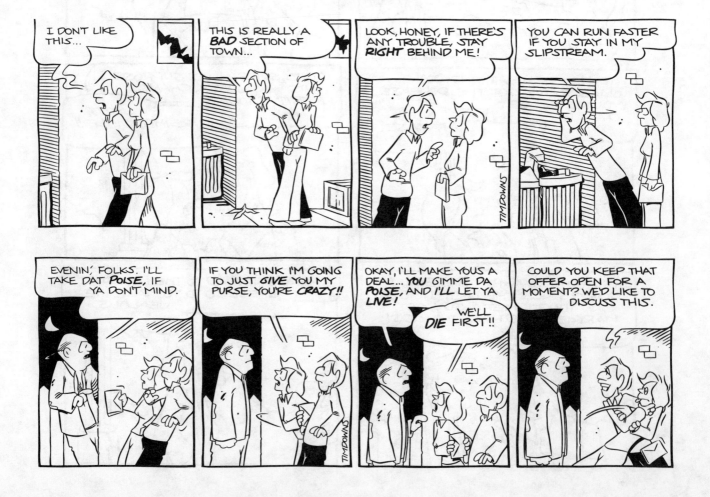

The inflated Ego also tends to shrink when exposed to another Ego of equal size. At least, it had better. How many inner tubes can you fit in the same trunk?

A relationship begins to decline when two Egos refuse to give way to each other. I call it "The Clash of the Titans."

The one change that would most radically improve our relationships would be the decision to deflate our Ego; to genuinely believe that the other person is at least as important as we are. Preferably more.

But sometimes the most obvious solutions prove to be the most difficult in practice.

What makes it so hard?

7 The Spirit

Sometimes in writing Dowstown I addressed the Big Issues: things like poverty and world hunger.

From time to time I even had the chance to address what I would consider the Biggest Issue.

Woody Allen was once asked how he felt now that he had achieved immortality through his work. He replied, "I'm not interested in achieving immortality through my work. I'm interested in achieving immortality through not dying." I'm with him.

All of our pursuits, including our relationships, are overshadowed by the brevity of life. Life is so busy that you can almost forget about it. But there always seem to be reminders.

One of my characters was a first grader named Malcom Magnesia. Nothing ever went right for Malcom. In these strips, Malcom represents a lot of people throughout history. Aware of his limitations, he tries desperately to build something that will last.

And like a lot of people throughout history, he finds that life often frustrates you.

The problem isn't simply one of brevity. It's also the question of Purpose. When the store closes in five minutes, you'd better know what you're shopping for.

If you don't know what you're shopping for, just grab anything. This is the founding principle of garage sales.

For a lot of people, it also seems to be their guiding principle in life.

Our fulfillment in life seems to depend on our ability to find an answer to the question of Purpose. Frankly, we could use some help.

The Ego, of course, would rather not have any help. It would rather answer the Big Questions by itself, and it takes great pride in its own answers. As someone once said, "Most people don't believe something because it's true; they think it's true because *they* believe it."

Human nature never seems to change, does it?

by Tim Downs

I SOLD MY SOUL TO MY CAREER.

MY WIFE IS FILING FOR DIVORCE. THE KIDS COULDN'T CARE LESS.

LAST WEEK I WAS FIRED FOR UNETHICAL BUSINESS PRACTICE.

I CAN'T EAT. I CAN'T SLEEP. THE CHEST PAINS ARE BACK.

BUT I DID IT MYYYY WAY!!

112

Each of us is like a small child at a ball game. If someone would lift us up, we could see what the score is. As it is, we're left staring at the back of some lady's hat.

To me, that's the Question of the Ages: "Is there someone who could lift me up, please?"

I've come to believe that there just might be.

   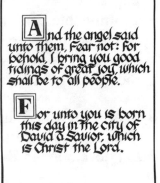

I was not required to go to church when I was growing up. I was glad. As Gallagher said, "I liked going to church when I was a kid. It reminded me that there was something more boring than school." That was my basic impression of all religion.

When I was in college, I met a group of people who called themselves Christians. I didn't care. Personally, I was a Virgo. What's in a name?

What I *did* care about was the quality of their lives. They seemed to have a confidence about life and a basic contentment with who they were. In a conversation, they didn't try to cram in as much information as possible about themselves. They were secure enough to ask questions, and to allow *me* to cram in as much information as possible about *myself.*

In other words, I saw a difference between their lives and mine.

They seemed firmly convinced of four things. First, that there is a God and that He is personal in nature. Second, that it's possible to find out reliable information about this God, and about His desires for our lives. Third, that it's not only possible to know *about* God, it's possible to know *God*—much like a human relationship. And fourth, that knowing God and gaining His perspective on life has a radical effect on the way you relate to other people.

From what I'd seen of the lives of these people, it was hard to argue.

To explain the concept of knowing God they gave me a helpful little booklet. The Bible can be a formidable book to an outsider. I had never opened one, except in high school to press my Prom boutonniere. In a dozen pages, this booklet managed to summarize the major themes of the New Testament. That's no small feat. With the author's permission, I have reproduced that little booklet for you in the Appendix of this book.

My Christian friends introduced me to the Bible, a book that has had a profound effect on my thinking, my writing and my relationships. It served as a springboard for many of the ideas I developed in **Downstown**. It continues to influence my life to this day.

In a book on relationships, I would do you a disservice if I did not recommend it.

by Tim Downs

8 Honesty and Commitment

In 1977 I saw the Woody Allen movie "Annie Hall." It was a landmark film. For the first time it allowed upper-middle class women to dress like street people.

Annie Hall, played by Diane Keaton, was having a serious relationship with Woody Allen, played by Woody Allen. Allen returned home to his New York apartment one day to find Annie Hall there, with all of her belongings.

He asked what she was doing. She said that she thought they could save a fortune by moving in together and getting rid of her apartment. He panicked.

He said, "Couldn't we just keep your apartment, sort of like a life raft, just so we'll know it's there?"

Our generation has a great fear of "the C-word": Commitment. We'd like to leave the back door open just a crack, so if the going gets tough, the tough can get going.

I think Honesty and Commitment are related. They both have to do with keeping promises; some are spoken, some are implied. Every relationship begins with a set of unspoken promises: a promise to tell the truth, to not manipulate or deceive, to protect personal trusts, and so on. The problem with dishonesty is that it gets us in the habit of breaking promises.

Dishonesty seems to creep into relationships unnoticed. Sometimes it takes the form of simple ploys.

Sometimes dishonesty is obvious. It's best that way. At least you know where you stand.

Sometimes dishonesty is a lot harder to spot. It's just a vague suspicion that this person is not what he seems to be, like those people in "Invasion of the Body Snatchers."

I was once standing in a check-out line with my two-year-old son. In front of us was a more-than-slightly overweight woman. My son said in a loud, clear voice, "Daddy, why is that woman so *fat*?" The woman turned and glared at *me*! I said, "This is a rented child."

Honesty means more than simply saying anything that comes to mind. It requires some tact. I like the way the Bible puts it: "Speak the truth in love." Truth supplies the content, love provides the packaging. That kind of honesty doesn't hurt.

Have you ever been going up an escalator, when a beautiful woman coming down on the opposite escalator catches your eye? A big smile comes across her face, and she waves cheerfully. You smile back, shout hello and blow her a kiss. Suddenly you realize that she isn't smiling at you at all, but at the Green Beret with the Rambo knife standing behind you.

That's what it feels like when you first suspect your partner has been dishonest about his commitment to you.

by Tim Downs

There's a natural fear of the Big Commitment for a number of reasons. First, you've seen a lot of relationships go down the tubes. It's enough to make you proceed with caution. A little fear can be a healthy thing.

Second, the Big Commitment gets a lot of bad press.

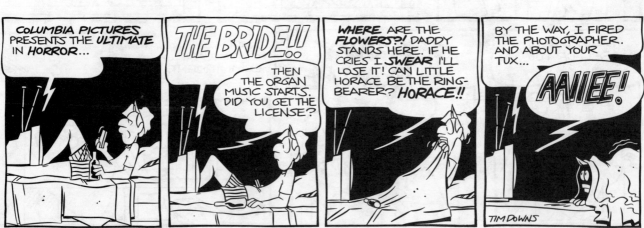

People today seem to feel that when you make a commitment, you lose something. It's like stepping into deep mud; you pull out your foot, and your shoe is gone.

Now there's an analogy that's destined for immortality.

As a result, we're quick to speak of a commitment, but slow to make one.

by Tim Downs

OH, *DONNA! DONNA!* LET ME *SHOW* YOU HOW MUCH I LOVE YOU!

OH YES! *SHOW* ME!

COMMIT YOURSELF TO MY WELFARE *REGARDLESS* OF THE COST TO YOU!

COMMUNICATE FREELY AND DEEPLY! SHARE YOUR DEEPEST DREAMS AND FEARS WITH ME!

SHOW A GENUINE CONCERN FOR THE PEOPLE AND THINGS THAT ARE IMPORTANT TO ME!

FORGIVE ME WHEN I'M WRONG WITHOUT KEEPING ACCOUNT OF MY OFFENSES AGAINST YOU!

DEFEAT YOUR PRIDE ENOUGH TO TAKE PLEASURE WHEN I AM HONORED OR PRAISED!

YES! SHOW ME!

UH... LET'S NOT GET CARRIED AWAY HERE...

TIM DOWNS

Someone has said, "A person who laughs at love is like a child who sings to himself in the dark." If no one has actually said this, now *I* have. You may quote me.

I hear people laugh at the idea of commitment. I wonder who they're trying to convince.

The most overused word in the English language is "love," with the possible exception of "impacting." "Love" is used so casually that its value has depreciated. We use it to mean very little, but often it still communicates a greater level of commitment than we intend. That can lead to trouble.

I think we need a new word. Any suggestions?

by Tim Downs

COMING TO BOOKSTORES THIS SUMMER... *FLIGHT OF FANCY!!*

HER MARRIAGE HAD BECOME A BORING MONOTONY OF DAILY NECESSITIES...

AND THEN ONE DAY SHE MET... *HIM!*

SHE WAS TORN BETWEEN HER WEDDING VOWS AND A WORLD SHE'D ONLY *DREAMED* OF... ...FOR ABOUT A MINUTE, THEN SHE SPLIT.

AND, OVER TIME, FOUND HER NEW RELATIONSHIP BECOMING MOSTLY A BORING MONOTONY OF DAILY NECESSITIES.

AFTER ALL, FOLKS, LIFE *IS* MOSTLY DAILY NECESSITIES.

NEW FROM *HARLEQUIN REALITIES.*

129

A woman told me a story about her two young daughters. The older one kicked the younger one, who began to cry. The mother said, "Why did you kick your sister?" Her daughter answered, "Because she kicked me back."

We all make mistakes in relationships. Why make excuses? I like this quotation: "A failure is simply a person who does not learn from his mistakes." But to learn from your mistakes, you first have to be willing to take responsibility for them.

Are Big Commitments a thing of the past? I doubt it. Something in the human spirit longs for them. But keeping them has never been easy. Something in the human spirit seems to assure that, too.

I suspect that the ability to make and keep Big Commitments is a key to the enjoyment of life as a whole. Unfortunately, Big Commitments require time and energy. They're costly.

But I suppose that shouldn't be a surprise. The best things in life are often costly.

Thought Bombs

Ten Challenging Thoughts on Relationships

1. Life *is* relationships.

2. Your happiness and fulfillment in life will largely be determined by your success or failure in relationships.

3. Anyone can succeed in a career by sacrificing all relationships. But Life is a juggling act. Anyone can juggle just one ball.

4. Our fear is not of commitment, but of slavery. They are opposites.

5. Sound relationships are made of sound people. A relationship is no stronger than the character of the individuals who comprise it.

6. Character is never an accident. The only person you can change in a relationship is you.

7. Relationships exist in three dimensions: your relationship to yourself, your relationship to others, and your relationship to God. They are intimately connected.

8. Excellence in any one of these three dimensions requires success in all of them. None can be ignored without harm.

9. We often expect too much from relationships. There are some needs no human being can meet.

10. The deepest human needs are met only in a relationship with God. The Question of the Ages is, "How is that relationship begun?"

Dear Friend,

Yes, you can know God personally, as presumptuous as that may sound. God is so eager to establish a personal, loving relationship with you that He has already made all the arrangements.

The major barrier that prevents us from knowing God personally is ignorance of who God is and what He has done for us. Read on and discover for yourself the joyful reality of knowing God personally.

> Bill Bright
> Founder and President
> Campus Crusade for Christ International

1 GOD **LOVES** YOU AND CREATED YOU TO KNOW HIM PERSONALLY.

(References contained in this booklet should be read in context from the Bible wherever possible.)

God's Love
"For God so loved the world, that He gave His only begotten Son, that whoever believes in Him should not perish, but have eternal life" (John 3:16).

God's Plan
"Now this is eternal life: that they may know you, the only true God, and Jesus Christ, whom you have sent" (John 17:3, NIV).

What prevents us from knowing God personally?

2 MAN IS **SINFUL** AND **SEPARATED** FROM GOD, SO WE CANNOT KNOW HIM PERSONALLY OR EXPERIENCE HIS LOVE.

Man Is Sinful
"For all have sinned and fall short of the glory of God" (Romans 3:23).

Man was created to have fellowship with God; but, because of his stubborn self-will, he chose to go his own independent way, and fellowship with God was broken. This self-will, characterized by an attitude of active rebellion or passive indifference, is evidence of what the Bible calls sin.

Man Is Separated

"For the wages of sin is death" (spiritual separation from God) (Romans 6:23).

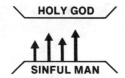

This diagram illustrates that God is holy and man is sinful. A great gulf separates the two. The arrows illustrate that man is continually trying to reach God and establish a personal relationship with Him through his own efforts, such as a good life, philosophy or religion.

The third principle explains the only way to bridge this gulf . . .

3 JESUS CHRIST IS GOD'S **ONLY** PROVISION FOR MAN'S SIN. THROUGH HIM ALONE WE CAN KNOW GOD PERSONALLY AND EXPERIENCE HIS LOVE.

He Died in Our Place

"But God demonstrates His own love toward us, in that while we were yet sinners, Christ died for us" (Romans 5:8).

He Rose From the Dead

"Christ died for our sins . . . He was buried . . . He was raised on the third day, according to the Scriptures . . . He appeared to Peter, then to the twelve. After that He appeared to more than five hundred . . ." (1 Corinthians 15:3-6).

He Is the Only Way to God

"Jesus said to him, 'I am the way, and the truth, and the life; no one comes to the Father, but through Me'" (John 14:6).

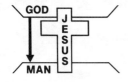

This diagram illustrates that God has bridged the gulf which separates us from Him by sending His Son, Jesus Christ, to die on the cross in our place to pay the penalty for our sins.

It is not enough just to know these truths . . .

4 WE MUST INDIVIDUALLY **RECEIVE** JESUS CHRIST AS SAVIOR AND LORD; THEN WE CAN KNOW GOD PERSONALLY AND EXPERIENCE HIS LOVE.

We Must Receive Christ

"But as many as received Him, to them He gave the right to become children of God, even to those who believe in His name" (John 1:12).

We Receive Christ Through Faith

"For by grace you have been saved through faith; and that not of yourselves, it is the gift of God; not as a result of works, that no one should boast" (Ephesians 2:8,9).

When We Receive Christ, We Experience a New Birth. (Read John 3:1-8.)

We Receive Christ by Personal Invitation

(Christ is speaking): "Behold I stand at the door and knock; if anyone hears My voice and opens the door, I will come into him" (Revelation 3:20).

Receiving Christ involves turning to God from self (repentance) and trusting Christ to come into our lives to forgive our sins and to make us the kind of people He wants us to be. Just to agree intellectually that Jesus Christ is the Son of God and that He died on the cross for our sins is not enough. Nor is it enough to have an emotional experience. We receive Jesus Christ by faith, as an act of the will.

These two circles represent two kinds of lives:

SELF-DIRECTED LIFE	CHRIST-DIRECTED LIFE
S—Self is on the throne	†—Christ is in the life and on the throne
†—Christ is outside the life	S—Self is yielding to Christ
●—Interests are directed by self, often resulting in discord and frustration	●—Interests are directed by Christ, resulting in harmony with God's plan

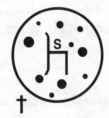 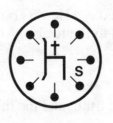

Which circle best represents your life?
Which circle would you like to have represent your life?
The following explains how you can invite Jesus Christ into your life.

YOU CAN RECEIVE CHRIST RIGHT NOW BY FAITH THROUGH PRAYER

(Prayer is talking with God)

God knows your heart and is not so concerned with your words as He is with the attitude of your heart. The following is a suggested prayer:

"Lord Jesus, I want to know You personally. Thank You for dying on the cross for my sins. I open the door of my life and receive You as my Savior and Lord. Thank You for forgiving my sins and giving me eternal life. Take control of the throne of my life. Make me the kind of person You want me to be."

Does this prayer express the desire of your heart?

If it does, pray this prayer right now, and Christ will come into your life, as He promised.

How to Know That Christ Is in Your Life.
Did you receive Christ into your life? According to His promise in Revelation 3:20, where is Christ right now in relation to you? Christ said that He would come into your life and be your friend so you can know Him personally. Would He mislead you? On what authority do you know that God has answered your prayer? (The trustworthiness of God Himself and His Word.)

The Bible Promises Eternal Life to all Who Receive Christ
"And the witness is this, that God has given us eternal life, and this life is in His Son, He who has the Son has the life; he who does not have the Son of God does not have the life. These things I have written to you who believe in the name of the Son of God, in order that you may know that you have eternal life" (1 John 5:11-13).

Thank God often that Christ is in your life and that He will never leave you (Hebrews 13:5). You can know on the basis of His promise that Christ lives in you and that you have eternal life, from the very moment you invite Him in. He will not deceive you.

A version of the Four Spiritual Laws, written by Bill Bright. Copyright 1965, 1988, Campus Crusade for Christ.
Reprinted by permission.

About *Downstown*

Tim Downs created **Downstown** in 1975 as a junior at Indiana University. It was published as a daily feature in the Indiana Daily Student and in other college newspapers until 1980, when it began syndication with Universal Press Syndicate.

The comic strips contained in this book appeared in North American newspapers between 1984 and 1986.

In 1986, Tim Downs retired his comic strip. He now works full-time with Campus Crusade for Christ, an organization of extremely enjoyable people.

The character of Joy in the comic strip was named after a woman he dated in college. He proposed marriage, under the threat of having her character run over by a car. She relented, and they were married in 1981. They currently live in Southern California with their three children.

For the sake of posterity, the final **Downstown** comic strip is reprinted below.